ARD
UGH

BRYAN
ROBSON

WALTER
ZENGA

RUUD GULLIT

TONY ADAMS

JAN CEULEMANS

STEVE BULL

JOHN

FRANK RIJKAARD

RONALD KOEMAN

IAN RUSH

CHRIS WADDLE

PETER BEARDSLEY

VE
OL

SCOIGNE

HUGO SANCHEZ

TONY ADAMS

ENGLAND

TONY ADAMS

ARSENAL

Club History
1983– Arsenal
Honours & Awards
Littlewoods Cup 1987
PFA Young Player of the Year 1987
League Championship 1989

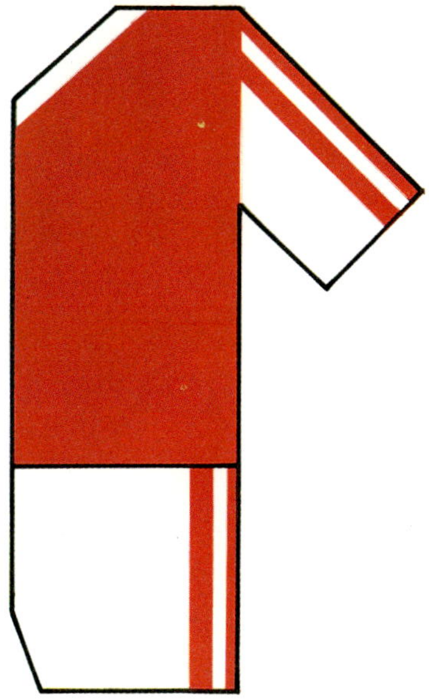

Tony Adams has been a tower of strength in the Arsenal team in recent years as they have challenged Liverpool's superiority in English football. The 6ft 1in, 13 stone central defender has been solid at the heart of the Gunners' defence and his inspirational ability was an important part of their drive to the First Division championship in 1988–89.

Tony was born in London on 10 October 1966, shortly after England's World Cup triumph. He joined Arsenal as an apprentice and made his senior debut against Sunderland in November 1983, but he failed to gain a regular first team place for three seasons, despite winning England Youth and Under-21 honours.

The 1986–87 season was an important one for Adams. He played in all of Arsenal's 42 League games and eventually gained the international recognition that many had been tipping him for. Bobby Robson made him the 998th player to appear for England when he played Adams in the friendly with Spain in Madrid in February 1987. With Wright and Watson both out injured, Tony got the chance and became, at the age of 20, the youngest centre-half to play for England.

Comparisons have been made between Adams and Bobby Moore. He has the same composure as Moore, despite being a rugged defender as opposed to a midfield player. But many have rightly predicted a long England career for the Arsenal player, just as they had done for Moore some years earlier.

Seven weeks after his international debut he was at the heart of the Arsenal defence which beat Liverpool 2–1 to win the Milk Cup at Wembley; the club's first honour since winning the FA Cup in 1979. It was a truly memorable ending to Adams' appearance as a first-team regular. Furthermore, he was the PFA's Young Player of the Year.

Since then, Tony has missed only a handful of games and his arrival in the Arsenal team has coincided with Arsenal's challenge to Liverpool's dominance. And in 1988–89 he guided the club to their first championship since 1971 when they beat the Anfield side with a goal in the closing seconds of the season.

Tony Adams is still only 24 but has shown a maturity well beyond his years. He is an excellent reader of the game and a great inspiration on the field. Both Arsenal and England are grateful for his presence.

JOHN BARNES

As Liverpool set about re-styling their attack in 1987, they saw the exciting John Barnes as an ideal newcomer. He fitted into the job well. Furthermore, he became a great favourite with the Anfield fans who, over the years, have had a long line of heroes. Barnes became another of them. And the fact that he was voted Player of the Year by both the Football Writers and his fellow professionals at the end of this first season at Anfield underlines what an impact he made at Liverpool.

John Barnes has all the attributes required of a goal-scoring forward. He has remarkable ball control and can take on defenders. He is not frightened to run at defences and many a defender has been left trailing by one of Barnes' famous dribbles. Once he has the target in sight he has a lethal shot to add powerful finishing to his great all-round game.

Born in Kingston, Jamaica, in November, 1963, John's father was an army officer and

ENGLAND

JOHN BARNES

Club History
1981–87 Watford
1987– Liverpool (£900,000)
Honours & Awards
League Championship 1988, 1990
FA Cup 1989
FWA & PFA Footballer of the Year 1988
FWA Footballer of the Year 1990

LIVERPOOL

also the skipper and later the coach of the Jamaican national team. John and his family came to England in 1976. He was spotted playing football for the Middlesex side Sudbury Court by the ex-Arsenal boss Bertie Mee and was snapped up by Watford. Two months after turning professional, he made his first team debut against Oldham Athletic in September 1981.

He scored 13 goals in his first season as Watford continued their remarkable run up the Football League and into the First Division for the first time in their history. The following season they took the top flight by storm and came close to winning the title but had to content themselves with the runner's-up position to Liverpool. But 'Barnsey' played a very important role in Watford's title challenge and complemented the great goal-scoring talents of Luther Blissett.

From the Fourth Division to First in four years was a remarkable achievement. But in 1984 Watford had more in store for their fans: a first Wembley FA Cup Final appearance. But they came up against a revitalised Everton team and John Barnes and his team-mates could not cope with their opponents who ran out 2–0 winners.

John had three more seasons at Watford and scored 65 goals in 233 League games for the Hertfordshire club. But the call of Liverpool was too great a temptation despite his southern roots, and in July 1987 a cheque for £900,000 captured his services. On 15 August he made his League debut for the Reds in the 2–1 win at Arsenal, along with another new boy, Peter Beardsley.

Liverpool won the League that season but John missed out on a cup winners' medal again when, this time, Wimbledon spoilt the celebrations. But in 1989 he eventually got the medal at the third attempt as Liverpool beat Everton in one of the game's most emotional cup finals in the wake of the Hillsborough disaster.

A regular member of Bobby Robson's England team, he has won around 50 caps but, despite the odd flash of brilliance, has not been able to consistently produce his Liverpool form in an England jersey. John Barnes is always capable of turning a game with one flash of brilliance. He does that all too often.

MARCO VAN BASTEN

Marco van Basten's arrival as one of the world's top strikers has coincided with Holland's emergence as a top international nation, and also AC Milan's revived fortunes in Europe.

Not only is van Basten a lethal striker of the ball with lightning-fast reflexes, but he is also an excellent target man and is capable of holding on to the ball and causing confusion amongst defences.

Born in Utrecht on 31 October 1964 he was signed by the great Ajax side when he was only 17, having established himself with the little known Elinwijk team. When he made his first team debut it was as a substitute for Ajax's favourite son, Johann Cruyff, three times winner of the European Footballer award.

Van Basten first entered the international stage as a member of the Dutch side which competed in the World Youth Tournament in Mexico in 1983. In the following four seasons he was Ajax's top scorer and on two occasions topped the 30 mark. His 37 goals in 1986 made him the top goal-scorer in Europe. During his five-year spell at Ajax he scored no fewer than 128 times. It was goal-scoring like that which attracted the top Italian club AC Milan who were hungry for European glory. And in 1987 their manager Arrigo Saachi splashed out a reported £3.3 million for the 22-year-old Dutchman.

Shortly before the move he scored the only goal of the game in the European Cup Winners' Cup Final against Lokomotiv Leipzig in Athens. Van Basten was Ajax captain that day and it was fitting that he should skipper the club to its first European success since the great glory days of Johann Cruyff in the early 1970s.

AC Milan were hoping that van Basten,

HOLLAND

MARCO VAN BASTEN

Club History
1981–87 Ajax
1987– AC Milan (£3,300,000)
Honours & Awards
Dutch Cup 1981, 1986, 1987
Dutch League 1982, 1983, 1985
Adidas Golden Boot Winner 1986
European Cup Winners' Cup 1987
European Championship 1988
European Footballer of the Year 1988, 1989
European Cup 1989
European Super Cup 1989

A C MILAN

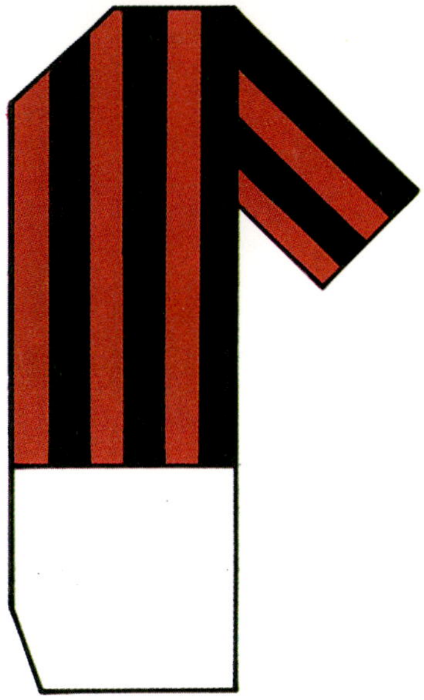

and their other expensive signing, Ruud Gullit, could bring back similar European glories to the once famous Italian side.

Twice winners of the European Cup, AC hadn't won the coveted trophy since 1969. In fact, their last success in Europe was in the 1973 Cup Winners' Cup. The same year Ajax last won the European Cup.

Sadly, van Basten was injured early in the 1987–88 season and missed most of the campaign which saw AC Milan capture the Italian League title. But surprisingly, despite missing most of the domestic season, van Basten was back to his immaculate best for the European Championship in West Germany.

He arrived in Germany having scored six goals in 18 international matches. By the time the tournament was over he had nearly doubled his goals tally as he ended up the top scorer with five.

Holland duly won the tournament with a magnificent display of all-round teamwork as well as individual brilliance from the likes of van Basten and Gullit.

Although he started the tournament on the subs' bench, van Basten soon set the tournament alight with a hat-trick against England, despite nursing a fractured cheek bone. It was Peter Shilton's 100th game for England, but one he would rather forget.

A last minute van Basten goal in the semi-final against West Germany eliminated the hosts, and pre-tournament favourites. But he saved his best goal for the final itself.

Already one up from a first-half Gullit goal, van Basten sealed the fate of the Soviets when he latched on to a Muhren cross from the left. Van Basten stood on the right of the penalty area at an acute angle as he hit a majestic volley which sailed past the Russian 'keeper Dassaev. The 2–0 victory gave Holland their first success at international level after many years of coming close. Van Basten's exploits earned him the European Footballer of the Year award for 1988, thus emulating his mentor, Johann Cruyff.

Back in Italy, Marco helped his Milan team to that much sought after European Cup success in 1989 when AC enjoyed a comfortable 4–0 win over Steaua Bucharest in the final. Van Basten scored two of Milan's goals. But that is Marco van Basten's trademark – scoring goals.

PETER BEARDSLEY

From reject to Britain's costliest footballer. That was the road Liverpool's Peter Beardsley took.

The diminutive Beardsley, the man who could do with a couple of front teeth for Christmas, was born in Newcastle-upon-Tyne on 18 January 1961. He had unsuccessful trials with Gillingham, Oxford, Burnley and Cambridge United and was resigned to playing local soccer for the Wallsend Boys Club when he was spotted by a local talent scout. He was recommended to former Newcastle player Bobby Moncur, who was manager of Carlisle United at the time, and Moncur took him under his wing in August 1979. The transfer fee – a new set of shirts for the Wallsend team!

Beardsley immediately went into the first team and made his debut in the 1–1 home draw with Blackburn Rovers on 21 August 1979. Sadly, Carlisle were forced to sell him for financial reasons. And after 102 games for the Brunton Park team he went to Vancouver Whitecaps for £250,000. But, despite playing alongside such household names as David Harvey, Terry Yorath, Peter Lorimer, Ray Hankin, and other well-known British players, Beardsley was out in the wilderness. He wanted English League soccer. However, it looked as though he was about to make the big breakthrough when Manchester United manager, Ron Atkinson, invited him to Old Trafford for a trial period in 1982. But it didn't work out and Peter's only appearance in the famous red shirt of United was in the Football League Cup match with Bournemouth. Even then he didn't play the whole match. So, it was rejection for the Geordie lad yet again, and it was back to Vancouver.

In September 1983 he eventually made the move which was to change his career. His home-town club Newcastle United had recently recruited the services of Kevin Keegan. The city was buzzing with excitement and several big name signings

ENGLAND

PETER BEARDSLEY

Club History
1979–82 Carlisle United
1982–83 Vancouver Whitecaps (£250,000)
1983 Manchester United (trial period)
1983–87 Newcastle United (£120,000)
1987– Liverpool (£1,900,000)
Honours & Awards
League Championship 1988, 1990
FA Cup 1989

LIVERPOOL

were complemented with that of Beardsley, who joined them for £120,000. Newcastle were prepared to give him his chance when others were not. And he took it. In his first season at St James's Park he scored 20 goals in 35 games as Newcastle won promotion to the First Division. The Keegan–Beardsley partnership was a great success, and was complemented by the fast-improving Chris Waddle.

But would Beardsley still be able to score goals in the First Division? The answer to that question was 'yes'. And his great goal-scoring exploits earned him international recognition. In January 1986 he made his England debut in the 4–0 win over Egypt. It was part of England's build-up to the World Cup in Mexico and Beardsley accepted his chance and was included in the squad for the finals.

After a dismal start to the tournamant, the England team was re-shuffled for the Poland game and Beardsley teamed up with Gary Lineker. It proved to be one of the best strike forces England had seen for a long time. Suddenly England were a different team and there was even talk of them winning the trophy. That's before the 'Hand of God' (or should that be 'Hand of Maradona'?) intervened.

Beardsley's return to the domestic game was marred by a season of injuries and he scored only five goals in 32 League games. Despite his dismal season, Liverpool had been eyeing him up and in the summer of 1987 went into lengthy negotiations. Eventually they got their man, as they often do, and Peter Beardsley became Britain's costliest footballer at £1.9 million.

He made his Liverpool debut in the 2–1 win at Highbury on the opening day of the 1987–88 season and became an instant hit with the Anfield fans who adored his delicate skills in the penalty area and his pin-point accurate passes.

His first season at Anfield yielded a League Championship medal and the following season he was in the Liverpool team which beat Everton 3–2 after extra time to win the FA Cup. Not a bad haul for a player who had failed trials at four clubs and had been rejected by Manchester United.

STEVE BULL

Just when we thought the mould that gave us such great goal-scorers as Nat Lofthouse, Denis Law and Jimmy Greaves had been thrown away, along came Steve Bull to remind us of the 'Good Old Days' of goal-scoring centre-forwards. Remember them? They were the guys who shot on sight and had an insatiable appetite for scoring goals. That's all Steve Bull wants to do – score goals.

Born at Tipton in the West Midlands in 1965, he started his career as an apprentice with West Bromwich Albion but they let him go to nearby Wolverhampton Wanderers in 1986.

He had made his debut for Albion at the back end of the 1985–86 season and scored the first of his many League goals during the following campaign when he netted twice against Ipswich. Paul Cooper, the Ipswich 'keeper, had the distinction of being the first man to concede a Bull goal. He was just the first of many!

When Bull made his Wolves debut in the 3–0 home win over Wrexham they were ninth in the Fourth Division. By the beginning of the year things had got worse and they were lying 17th in the table, a desperate

ENGLAND

STEVE BULL

Club History
1985–86 West Bromwich Albion
1986– Wolverhampton Wanderers
Honours & Awards
Fourth Division 1987
Sherpa Van Trophy 1987
Third Division 1988

WOLVES

position for a once famous Midlands club.

But then the Bull goal-scoring machine suddenly came to life. He scored 12 goals in the last 21 games which saw Wolves end up in fourth place and in the play-offs. Unfortunately, Aldershot beat them in the final and so it was another season in the Fourth Division. But Wolves were about to rediscover their former glories and start the move towards the top division where they belong.

In 44 League games Bull scored a staggering 34 goals. In all games he scored a club record 52 goals as Wolves swept to the Fourth Division title. They also made a Wembley appearance when they beat Burnley in front of an 80,000 crowd to win the Sherpa Van Trophy. Surprisingly, Bull didn't score on the arena which many thought would be suited to his style of play.

Bull proved that he could score goals after stepping up a division and he even improved on his total to score 37 goals in the League as Wolves won the Third Division championship. His overall total was again over 50. Goal-scoring of that nature hadn't been seen for a long time and understandably the big clubs were taking note. But Bull was having none of it. He loves his Black Country roots and is loyal to Wolves. Nothing would please him more than to score goals for Wolves in the First Division.

But it was not only the First Division managers who had their eyes on Bull. England manager Bobby Robson was also taking note of the new goal-scoring sensation and the Under-21 and 'B' international was promoted to the senior team for the game against Scotland at Hampden Park in 1989.

He was one of the substitutes and came on to the field as a replacement for John Fashanu after 31 minutes. England were one up at the time but the Scottish defence knew they were in for all sorts of problems once Bull came on. Bull ran for the goal and hit whenever he had the target in vision and in the 80th minute he was rewarded with a truly great goal, his 55th of the season, to crown a truly great debut. Alex McLeish, the established Scottish defender said afterwards: "The worst thing that happended to us was John Fashanu going off." And that probably echoes the sentiments of defenders up and down Britain when playing against Bull.

JAN CEULEMANS

BELGIUM

JAN CEULEMANS

Club History
1975–78 FC Lierse
1978– FC Bruges (£250,000)
Honours & Awards
Belgian Footballer of the Year 1980, 85, 88
Belgian League 1980, 1988
Belgian Cup 1986

F C BRUGES

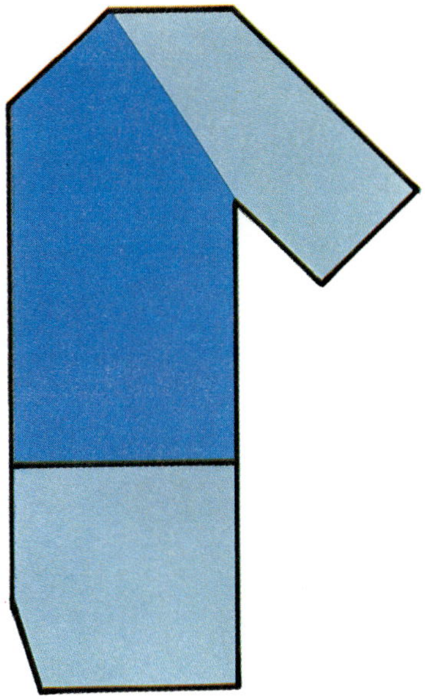

Jan Ceulemans is one of the finest footballers ever produced by Belgium and he has remained loyal to his homeland and resisted the temptation of the lira and peseta to take his skills to either Italy or Spain.

He was born in 1957 and is still a very prominent member of the Belgian national side. He won his first cap as a 20-year-old in 1977 and in September 1989 he surpassed Paul Van Himst's record of 81 caps. Now approaching his 90th appearance for Belgium, Jan has every chance of joining the elite '100 club'.

Tall, at 6ft 2in, he spent many years as a striker but in recent years has reverted to an attacking left-sided midfield role.

A youth international since 1976, he began his career with the Belgian First Division side FC Lierse before his move to FC Bruges in 1978. The fee was a then Belgian record £250,000.

Since joining Bruges he has remained tremendously loyal to them and it was unfortunate that he missed out on their European Cup Final appearance against Liverpool in 1978 when he was absent through injury. His delicate skills could just have swayed the game in favour of the Belgians who lost out to a solitary Kenny Dalglish goal.

Despite winning the Belgian League twice, and the Cup once, since Jan joined them, Bruges haven't appeared in another European final.

But it has been at international level where Jan has shown his world class. And in the 1980 European Championship he was outstanding as Belgium became the surprise finalists but lost 2–1 to West Germany. He scored Belgium's goal in the 1–1 draw with England in their group match. Belgium were not as successful in the 1982 and 1986 World Cup competitions, although Jan was a vital member of both squads.

The man who has been loyal to Belgian football has been duly rewarded and was Belgian Footballer of the Year in 1980, 1985 and 1988. He still has a few years in front of him and can look forward to the 1990s with relish as he strives to become the first Belgian to represent his country 100 times.

PAUL GASCOIGNE

When Paul Gascoigne joined Tottenham Hotspur from Newcastle United in the summer of 1988, he took Terry Venables' spending over the £6.5 million mark in the eight months he had been manager at White Hart Lane. 'Gazza' cost a cool £2 million which made him Britain's costliest footballer at the time. But Venables

ENGLAND

PAUL GASCOIGNE

TOTTENHAM

Club History
1984–88 Newcastle United
1988– Tottenham Hotspur (£2,000,000)
Honours & Awards
PFA Young Player of the Year 1988

knew that he was the sort of creative midfield player who would fit into his new-look team. Furthermore, Gascoigne is one of the game's characters and clubs need such players.

Despite having the chance of joining Manchester United, Gascoigne decided the new-look Spurs, which contained other new signings Terry Fenwick, Bobby Mimms, Paul Walsh and Paul Stewart, was more suited to him.

Like his new Spurs team-mate and former Newcastle United colleague Chris Waddle, Gascoigne was born in Gateshead, in 1967. He joined Newcastle as an apprentice and made his senior debut as a 17-year-old against QPR in April 1985.

The following season he earned himself a permanent place in the team and was the second highest scorer behind Peter Beardsley with nine goals. After the signing of Paul Goddard from West Ham the following season, Gascoigne was out of the team, but he returned in the latter part of the season, coincidentally against Spurs. In the close season, however, he figured in Dave Sexton's plans and was a member of the England team that competed in the UEFA Under-21 tournament in Toulon.

After another season with Newcastle, Gascoigne made the move to London and teamed up with his ex-Newcastle colleague Waddle. A couple of months after the move he made his full England debut when he came on as substitute for his former Newcastle team-mate Peter Beardsley in the friendly with Denmark at Wembley in September 1988.

To end a memorable year for Gascoigne, he was voted the PFA's Young Player of the Year for 1988. But sadly, on the field all was not going too well for the new Spurs side. The big investment was not showing immediate signs of paying off and Tottenham were languishing at the bottom of the table. Terry Venables, however, knew that such talented players as Waddle, Stewart, Walsh and Gascoigne would blend together and by the end of the season they were showing signs that it was all coming good and Spurs finished sixth in the table with 'Gazza' playing a big part in their revival.

RICHARD GOUGH

SCOTLAND

RICHARD GOUGH

RANGERS

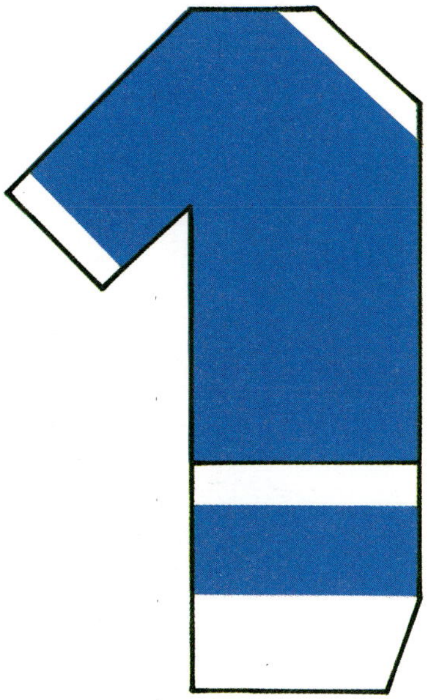

Club History
1981–86 Dundee United
1986–87 Tottenham Hotspur (£725,000)
1987– Glasgow Rangers (£1,500,000)
Honours & Awards
Scottish Premier Division 83, 89, 90
Scottish League Cup 1987–88, 1988–89

When Graeme Souness took Richard Gough to Ibrox in 1987 it cost the Rangers boss £1.5 million. He had tried to sign him prior to his move to Spurs but the irony is that Rangers had him on a week's trial when he was a youngster and could have had him for nothing. But they let him go. 'Funny 'ole game, football!'

Richard Gough is a solid defender who was born in Stockholm of a Swedish mother. Brought up in South Africa he started his footballing career there and was spotted while playing for the Witts University team before joining Dundee United in 1981. He made his United debut as a substitute on 22 April 1981 and played in the last four games of the season, all wearing the number 12 shirt.

Over the next five seasons he made the number four shirt his own property and missed only the occasional game. During United's 1982–83 championship season, their first ever, he missed just two matches. And he culminated a magnificent season at club level by winning the first of over 40 Scotland caps in the disappointing 2–2 draw with Switzerland at Hampden.

Richard was in Scotland's World Cup squad in 1986 but on his return joined Spurs after 255 appearances for Dundee United. Coincidentally his last game for United was against Rangers and the move to London was similar to the one his father Charlie made a few years earlier when he played for Charlton.

Gough's future at Spurs seemed assured. He signed a long-term contract, was made club captain, and was seen to be an ideal replacement for Spurs' failure to sign the England defender Terry Butcher during the summer. However, his stay at Spurs was short-lived, and a little over a year after his move south the homesick Gough was back in Scotland and playing for Rangers after a record deal involving a Scottish club. Another Scottish favourite, Frank McAvennie returned 'home' the same day following his move from West Ham.

Richard immediately settled in at his new club and a couple of months after the move he was in the Rangers side that beat Aberdeen to win the Skol Cup. Twelve months later it was a repeat win, followed by a second Championship medal later in the season to go with the one he won at Dundee United six years earlier.

RUUD GULLIT

There is no mistaking Ruud Gullit on the soccer field. He's the one with the dreadlock-type hairstyle. He's also the man with the brilliant ball control and lethal shooting skills.

Born in Amsterdam on 1 September 1962, of a Dutch mother and Surinamese father, he emerged in the second half of the 1980s as one of the game's finest players and was equal to the skills of his Latin counterparts.

Ruud Gullit started playing his football with an Under-8s team known as Merrboys before moving to DWS Amsterdam as a junior. He moved into the senior game with Haarlem in 1979 and made his Dutch League debut in August that year, a month short of his 17th birthday.

He celebrated his 19th birthday by making his senior international debut against Switzerland in September 1981. But it wasn't to be a happy birthday because the Swiss sprang a surprise and won 2–1. However, since then Gullit has gone on to win more than 40 caps – and mostly on the winning side.

A move to Feyenoord in 1982 saw him collect his first major domestic honours when he helped his new club to the League and Cup double in 1984. The following year he moved to PSV Eindhoven and in 1986 and 1987 they were Dutch champions, thanks largely to the influence of Gullit.

But talent like Gullit's is open to the targets of the powerful Italian and Spanish clubs and it was AC Milan who acquired his rare skills when they paid a staggering £5.5 million for him in the summer of 1987. With the acquisition of fellow Dutchman, Marco van

HOLLAND

RUUD GULLIT

Club History
1979–82 Haarlem
1982–85 Feyenoord
1985–87 PSV Eindhoven
1987– AC Milan (£5,500,000)
Honours & Awards
Dutch League 1984, 1986, 1987
Dutch Cup 1984
European Footballer of the Year 1987
Italian League 1988
European Championship 1988
European Cup 1989
European Super Cup 1989

A C MILAN

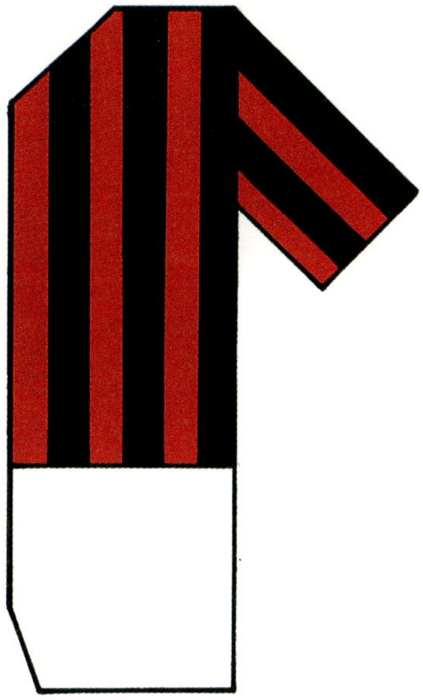

Basten, it took the Italian club's spending to nearly £9 million that summer. But that was the price they put on obtaining European Cup glory.

Gullit won the European Footballer of the Year award for 1987 and completed his first season in Italy with a championship winners' medal as AC won the Italian title for the first time since 1979. They were back on the European Cup trail. Before then, however, Gullit and his Dutch colleagues had the important matter of the European Championship in Germany to contend with.

The team, assembled by the shrewd manager Rinus Michels, was made up of brilliant individuals moulded together into a powerful unit. After losing their opening group match to the Soviet Union they then turned on the power with a 3–1 win over England. And after beating the hosts 2–1 in the semi-final they were up against Russia again in the Munich final.

Gullit saved his first goal of the tournament for the final when he scored after 33 minutes and set Holland on their way to winning their first major international trophy.

Having achieved international and domestic success in both Italy and Holland, Gullit was now keen to win himself a European Cup medal. And he played a very important role in AC Milan's route to the European Cup final in the 1988–89 season. But he very nearly missed the final.

Having virtually single-handedly destroyed Real Madrid in the semi-final, he was carried off injured. His right knee was severely damaged and should have had surgery. By his own admission he was only 60 per cent fit when he went into the final.

The final was played at Barcelona's Nou Camp stadium in front of 97,000 fans. But even they must have been surprised at the ease with which the Italians tore their Romanian opponents, Steaua Bucharest, apart. Two goals from Gullit and one from van Basten in the first half assured them of their third European Cup success. The victory was sealed by a second van Basten goal in the second half. In addition to his own two goals, Gullit hit the post once. What would the scoreline have been if he had been fully fit?

The £5.5 million investment of AC Milan had paid off and Ruud Gullit had proved once more that he was one of the game's finest footballers.

MARK HUGHES

On his day, Mark Hughes can be one of the most exciting footballers in Britain. And in front of goal he occasionally produces those flashes of brilliance the Old Trafford fans have come to expect over the years after being dished up such delights by the likes of George Best and Denis Law.

Mark was born at Wrexham, North Wales on 1 November 1963. He was snapped up by the United scouting system and he became an apprentice. He spent three years in the reserves, firstly as a midfielder, and then centre-forward, before getting his first-team chance when he came on as a substitute for Norman Whiteside in a Milk Cup tie against Port Vale in October 1983.

WALES

MARK HUGHES

Club History
1980–86 Manchester United
1986–88 Barcelona (£2,300,000)
(loan to Bayern Munich – 1988)
1988– Manchester United (£1,800,000)
Honours & Awards
FA Cup 1985, 1990
PFA Young Player of the Year 1985
PFA Footballer of the Year 1989

MANCHESTER UTD

The following month he made his second first-team appearance – in a European Cup Winners' Cup tie against Spartak Varna. However, it was not until the following March that he appeared in his first full League game, when he scored in the 2–0 win over Leicester City.

He missed only two more games that season and scored three more goals. A year later he was a virtual ever present and Mark made a meteoric rise to stardom that would soon take him into the £1 million transfer bracket.

Sixteen goals in the 1984–85 season made Mark United's top League scorer and against Aston Villa on 23 March he scored his first hat-trick. United finished fourth in the League but at Wembley they overcame the handicap of having Kevin Moran sent off to beat Everton 1–0 after extra time thanks to a Norman Whiteside goal. Mark collected his first winners' medal at Old Trafford.

Top scorer again the following season, Mark was showing great flair in the penalty area, not only for United but for Wales. He made his full international debut in May 1984. And what a debut it was! The game was played in front of his 'home' fans at Wrexham, and he scored the only goal of the game to beat England in the last match between the two countries in the International Championship.

Since then he has formed a formidable front-running partnership with Ian Rush and both have scored some memorable goals for their country. But none was more spectacular than Mark's overhead goal against Spain in a World Cup qualifier at Wrexham in 1985.

Terry Venables, the new Barcelona manager, had his eye on a couple of British exports during the summer of 1986 and he captured two of Britain's best goal-scorers in Gary Lineker and Mark Hughes.

Mark cost Barcelona £2.3 million, but his career abroad was an unhappy one. He didn't fit in at Barcelona and had a spell on loan at Bayern Munich before returning to Old Trafford in a £1.8 million deal in the summer of 1988. The United fans were glad to have him back and he was their top scorer again and was also voted the PFA's Footballer of the Year.

RONALD KOEMAN

Although a sweeper, Ronald Koeman has the habit of popping up to score some crucial goals, and in his last two seasons at Ajax scored no fewer than 37 goals. Some record for a defender.

Born in 1963 he began his career with Dutch First Division team FC Groningen in 1980, just as his father had done before him. His father is currently the Groningen trainer. Football certainly flows through the veins of the Koeman family because Ronald's older brother Erwin is a fellow Dutch international who now plays for Mechelen, the Belgian champions and European Cup Winners' Cup winners.

HOLLAND

RONALD KOEMAN

Club History
1980–83 FC Groningen
1983–86 Ajax
1986–89 PSV Eindhoven
1989– Barcelona (£4,800,000)
Honours & Awards
Dutch League 1985–89
Dutch Cup 1988, 1989
Dutch Footballer of the Year 1988
European Cup 1988
European Championship 1988
Spanish Cup 1990

BARCELONA

After three years at Groningen, Ronald was snapped up by the crack Dutch team Ajax and won a League championship medal with them in 1985. He made the move to PSV Eindhoven the following year and helped them to four consecutive Dutch League titles. He collected dual League and Cup medals in 1988 and 1989 and was a member of the PSV team which won the European Cup for the first time in 1988 when they beat Benfica 6–5 on penalties after a goal-less game.

Ronald had little opportunity to show his skills in a lacklustre game because he was heavily marked by the Benfica players. But a few months later both Ronald and brother Erwin were allowed to display their talents in West Germany as Holland sought to win their first major international honour at the European Championship.

After finishing second in their qualifying group to the Soviet Union, Holland met the host nation in the semi-final and fell behind to a Matthaus penalty in the 55th minute. But Ronald levelled the score 16 minutes from time when he also converted a spot-kick. As the game seemed to be heading for extra time that lethal goal-scorer Marco van Basten scored the match winner in the dying seconds of normal time and Holland were in the final against the Soviets, who had beaten them in their group match.

The Dutch didn't need reminding that they had been beaten in two World Cup Finals. But happily for them it was to be a case of third time lucky and they ran out 2–0 winners to win their first major honour at senior international level. For the Koeman brothers it was a great occasion, and for Ronald his year was completed with the Dutch Footballer of the Year award.

He spent just one more season with PSV before making the lucrative move to Spain where he joined Barcelona in a £4.8 million deal in the summer of 1989.

Koeman found it difficult to adapt at first and pressure was immediately on him because the Catalan side didn't have the best of starts in the Spanish League.

Ronald has the responsibility of taking Barcelona's free kicks and penalties and has a fearsome shot which will produce many goals for the Spaniards. He has now settled in well and hopefully will continue to win medals just as he did with Ajax and PSV.

OLEG KUZNETSOV

U S S R

OLEG KUZNETSOV

DYNAMO KIEV

Club History
1982– Dynamo Kiev
Honours & Awards
Soviet League 1985, 1986
European Cup Winners' Cup 1986

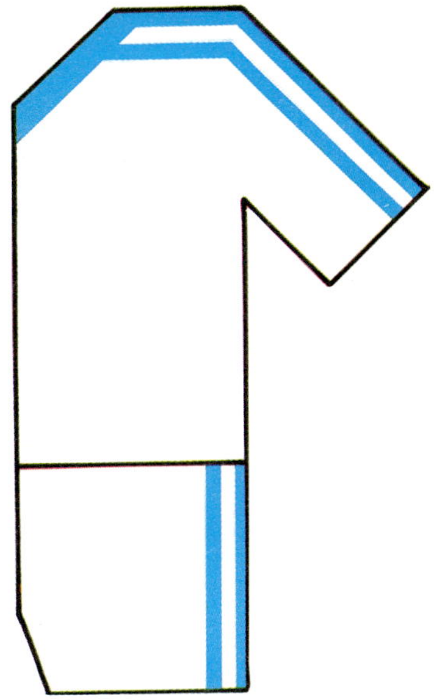

The Soviets confirmed their rise to the top of international soccer during the 1988 European Championship in West Germany. Sadly for central defender Oleg Kuznetsov he missed his country's finest hour. Because of a tackle on Italy's Valli which resulted in a yellow card in the semi-final he was ruled out of the final. Despite receiving a caution and knowing he would miss the final he still had a great game and set up Russia's opening goal in the 2–0 win over the Italians with one of his typical forceful runs.

But how he was missed in the final as Holland captured the trophy by two goals to nil. His inspirational powers were sadly missing. But despite being left out of the final, he was one of the outstanding players of the tournament.

Born in 1963 he started his career with junior teams in the Ukraine. He had already trained with Dynamo Kiev before his eventual permanent move in 1982. At the time most of the Soviet national squad were at Dynamo, and it would not be long before the name of Oleg Kuznetsov would be pencilled in on the international team sheet.

He won his first cap against Spain in January 1986 and was called into the 1986 World Cup as a stop-gap, but adequately lived up to his reputation. Since then he has been a regular and vital member of the national team and now has well over 40 caps to his name.

One of the greatest compliments Kuznetsov could have been paid was when he was sought after to play in the Italian League.

But, like most Soviet players, they tend not to move a great deal from one club to another, and he stayed at Dynamo Kiev. They won the Soviet championship in 1985 and 1986 and in the second of those years they won their first European honour when they beat Athletico Madrid 3–0 to win the European Cup Winners' Cup at Lyon. However, the Rumanian side Steau Bucharest spoilt Dynamo Kiev's chance of winning the Super Cup with a 1–0 win at Monaco.

Oleg Blochin was the first great Russian to be considered amongst the best in Europe. A decade later Igor Belanov was rightly regarded as one of Europe's top strikers. Both of them played for Dynamo Kiev. Now, the club has produced another player who can be regarded as one of Europe's finest, if not one of the world's best: Oleg Kuznetsov.

GARY LINEKER

When you look at the long list of talented players who started their career at Leicester City, it is perhaps surprising that the Midlands club has never won any of the sport's major trophies. Gary Lineker is just another of the very talented footballers to be born in Leicester and start his career with the Filbert Street club.

Born on 30 November 1960 he joined City as an apprentice and turned professional shortly after his 18th birthday.

He made his League debut against Oldham on New Year's Day 1979, but he had to wait until the end of the season before he was recalled for first team duty. Against Notts County on 24 April he scored the first of his 95 goals for Leicester.

He established himself as a first team regular in 1981–82 and was City's top scorer for the next four seasons, scoring over 20 League goals three seasons in succession.

England manager Bobby Robson needed the goal-scoring talents of Lineker as part of his rebuilding programme after failing to reach the 1984 European Championship finals, and Gary made his international debut in the 1–1 draw with Scotland in May 1984. Strangely, he didn't net his first goal for England until his

ENGLAND

GARY LINEKER

Club History
1977–85 Leicester City
1985–86 Everton (£800,000)
1986–88 Barcelona (£2,750,000)
1988– Tottenham Hotspur (£1,500,000)
Honours & Awards
Second Division 1980
PFA & FWA Footballer of the Year 1986
Spanish Cup 1988

TOTTENHAM

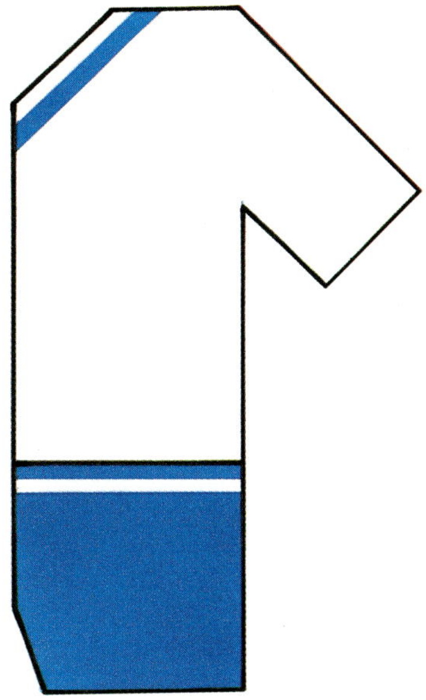

sixth match when he scored twice in the 5–0 win over the United States 12 months after making his debut. But since then he has gone on to become one of England's most prolific goal-scorers and has a very good chance of overtaking Bobby Charlton's all-time record of 49 goals.

Three goals against Turkey in a World Cup qualifier in 1985 were followed by another hat-trick against Poland during the 1986 World Cup finals in Mexico which revived England's apparent flagging fortunes. He scored twice in the next round against Paraguay and another in the 2–1 defeat by Argentina to take his World Cup tally to six.

Having emerged from the shadow of Liverpool, Merseyside neighbours Everton were prepared to splash out to bring the talented Lineker to Goodison Park and in the 1985 close season he was signed for £800,000.

In just one season at Everton he became a great favourite with the fans and scored 30 League goals as 'The Toffees' finished second to Liverpool in both the League and FA Cup. Gary, however, collected both the PFA and Football Writers' Player of the Year awards.

It was during his triumphant World Cup that Barcelona manager Terry Venables decided that Gary was the man required to add fire power to the Catalan team and a cheque for £2,750,000 took him to Spain. He became equally popular with the fans at the Nou Camp as he had been at Goodison Park and he soon showed he could score goals against the tight Spanish defences. He won a Spanish Cup winners' medal with his new club in 1988 but after Johann Cruyff returned to Barcelona as manager, Lineker fell out of favour with the new management team and in the summer of 1989 Terry Venables signed him a second time when he returned to England to join Spurs.

The Barcelona fans were against the move and a poll in a local newspaper revealed that more than 60 per cent of the fans wanted him to stay. But that's football.

Away from the football field Gary is an excellent snooker player and is capable of knocking in century breaks. It is hardly surprising really. One of his best friends, and playing partners, is the top snooker player Willie Thorne who was best man at Gary's wedding.

DIEGO MARADONA

Unquestionably the most naturally talented footballer in the world today is Diego Armando Maradona. He was born at Lanus, Argentina, on 30 October 1960. His outstanding skills were spotted by a talent scout who saw him playing for a local Buenos Aires youth team, Los Cebollitos – the Little Onions. The scout recommended Maradona to the then little known Argentine First Division team Argentinos Juniors.

Argentinos were duly impressed, not only

ARGENTINA

DIEGO MARADONA

Club History
1976–79 Argentinos Juniors
1979–82 Boca Juniors (£1,000,000)
1982–84 Barcelona (£5,000,000)
1984– Napoli (£6,900,000)
Honours & Awards
South American Footballer of the Year 1979, 1980
Spanish Cup 1983
World Footballer of the Year 1986
Italian League 1987
Italian Cup 1987
UEFA Cup 1989

NAPOLI

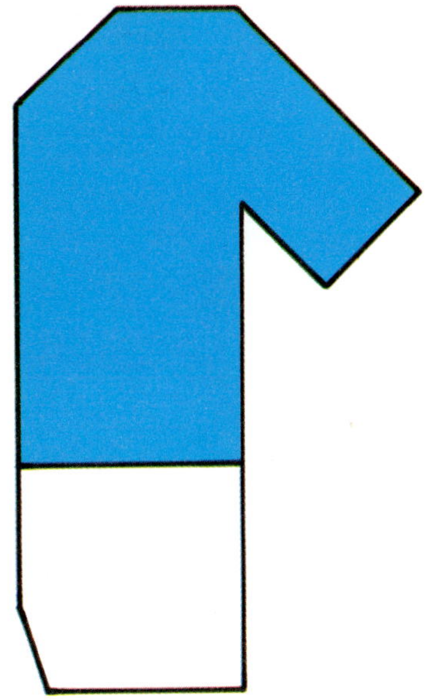

with Maradona, but with the whole team and they took the entire squad under their wing and incorporated them as one of their own youth teams!

In 1977 at the age of 16, Maradona gained his first international cap when he played for his country against Hungary and became Argentina's youngest ever international. Two years later he skippered his country to victory in the World Youth Cup in Japan. Shortly afterwards Maradona was transferred to the top Argentine club Boca Juniors for the equivalent of £1 million.

He was South American Player of the Year in 1979 and 1980, but his home country was to lose his delicate skills as the lure of the peseta was too great and a £5 million transfer took him to Barcelona in June 1982.

In his first season in Spanish football he helped Barcelona win the three major Spanish Cup competitions; the Spanish Cup, League Cup and Spanish Super Cup.

After two years with 'Barca' he moved to Italy where he joined Napoli in another world record transfer when the Italians paid £6.9 million for his services.

Napoli had never won the League championship in their long history and had failed to win the Cup since 1962. However, their investment paid off in 1987 when they captured both the League and Cup double.

A year earlier Maradona had skippered Argentina to their second World Cup success when they beat West Germany 3–2 in a thrilling final in the Azteca Stadium, Mexico City. It was Maradona who was the scourge of England in the quarter-finals when he put paid to their chances with two goals including the now famous and dubious 'Hand of God' goal . . . or should that read the 'Hand of Maradona' goal?

Voted the World Footballer of the Year for 1986, the tiny Argentinian with the immaculate ball control, balance and body swerve, is now a firm favourite with his Napoli fans and in 1989 he helped the club to their first ever success in Europe when they beat the German side Stuttgart to win the UEFA Cup.

Despite a temporary absence from the club at the start of the 1989–90 season, Maradona patched up his differences with club officials and returned to wear their shirt once more and continued doing what he enjoys best – weaving his way through defences and scoring goals.

ALLY McCOIST

SCOTLAND

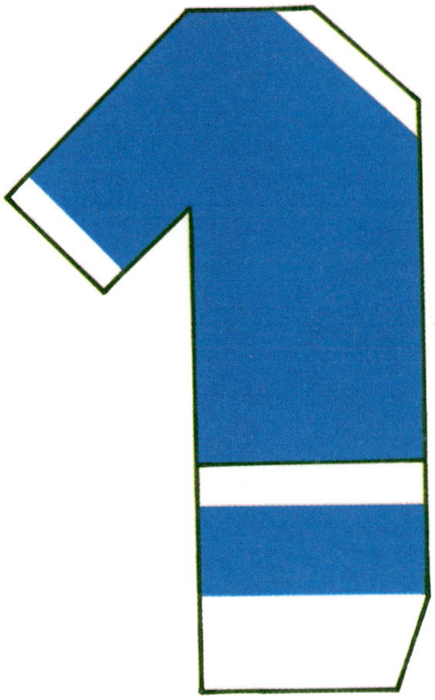

ALLY McCOIST

Club History
1978–81 St Johnstone
1981–83 Sunderland (£300,000)
1983– Glasgow Rangers (£185,000)
Honours & Awards
Scottish League Cup 1983–84, 1984–85, 1986–87, 1987–88, 1988–89
Scottish Premier Division 87, 89, 90

RANGERS

In the years since Graeme Souness took charge at Ibrox, many of the men who have worn the blue jersey of the famous club have come from south of the border. But one notable exception has been Ally McCoist, one of the most lethal strikers in Scotland.

Born in the Belshill district of Glasgow in 1962, Ally first attracted attention when he moved from junior Lanarkshire football to St Johnstone in 1978. But he made only 19 appearances in the League in his first two seasons at Muirton Park. However, he became a regular first-teamer in 1980–81 and scored 22 goals in 38 matches. It was goal-scoring like that which was to, inevitably, take him away from St Johnstone. Despite offers from Rangers' manager John Greig, McCoist decided to move south and he joined Sunderland in a £300,000 deal in 1981.

But just eight goals in 56 League games at Roker Park marked a frustrating period in the career of Ally McCoist and in June 1983 Rangers eventually got their man, this time for a mere £185,000. Twelve months earlier they had bid £300,000 for him but this was £100,000 short of Sunderland's valuation. It obviously pays to wait!

Although he struggled to find his goal-scoring touch at first, the hat-trick he scored in the 1983 League Cup final against Celtic to win the trophy in extra time was ample compensation.

The goal-scoring returned and he netted 24 League goals in the 1985–86 season with 33 goals in Rangers' championship season a year later, the first under Souness' managership. His hat-trick against Hearts at the end of the season surpassed Jim Forrest's post-war club record. And between them, the Rangers strike force of McCoist and Fleck scored 52 goals that season.

Unfortunately, a hamstring injury forced McCoist to miss a large part of Rangers' next championship season 1988–89, but shortly before he was side-lined he scored the winner in Rangers' 3–2 victory over Aberdeen in the Skol Cup final. It was Ally's fifth winners' medal.

Ally had been called up by Scotland team boss Alex Ferguson for his international debut against Holland in April 1986 and to date has won nearly 20 caps. His alertness in front of goal makes him one of the sharpest forwards in Scotland.

STEVE NICOL

An essential quality of a player joining Liverpool FC is often patience. Over the years they have signed players from lower divisions, but have refused to unleash them in to the first-team until the club's management felt the time was right. Ian Rush is a prime example and another is defender Steve Nicol. His patience has, however, been rewarded and he is now a crucial member of the Liverpool and Scotland squads.

Born at Irvine, Scotland, in December 1961, Steve joined Scottish League side Ayr United from a local boys club team and made his debut in the 2–1 home win over Arbroath in October 1979. It was in 1980

SCOTLAND

STEVE NICOL

Club History
1979–81 Ayr United
1981– Liverpool (£300,000)
Honours & Awards
European Cup 1984
League Championship 84, 86, 88, 90
FA Cup 1986, 1989
FWA Footballer of the Year 1989

LIVERPOOL

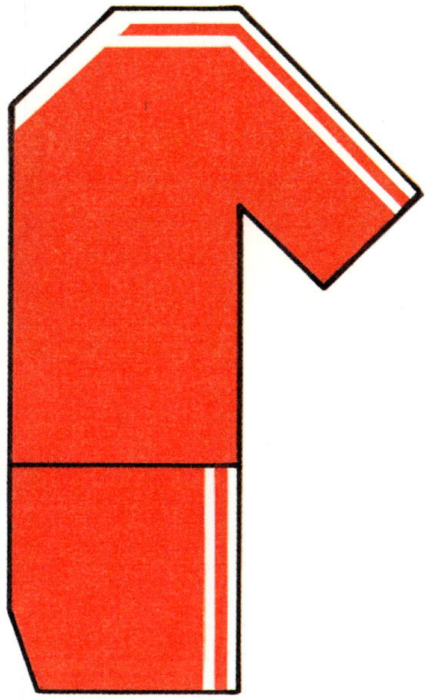

that he made the left-back position his own. An ever-present the following season, Liverpool scouts had been keeping an eye on him and midway through the 1981–82 season the Anfield club paid £300,000 for the little-known player south of the border.

He completed his Anfield apprenticeship in the club's highly successful Central League side and continued to gain representative honours as a Scottish Under-21 international. He went on to beat Ray Stewart's record of 12 caps for the Under-21s.

Nicol was given his Football League debut in the 2–0 win at Highbury in September 1982 when he was played in the right-back role. But it was three months before he was given another chance. He played just two more games that season, both as substitute, and remarkably he still hadn't appeared in a League game at Anfield. All four matches were away.

The following season he got his chance to take over the right midfield role when Craig Johnston injured a shoulder at Queen's Park Rangers. Nicol came on for the injured Johnston, and scored the only goal of the game seven minutes from time. The Scot was given Johnston's place in the team and when Craig returned to the side a few weeks later, Steve kept his place in the team.

He lost his position to Ronnie Whelan in the second half of the season but was one of the substitutes for the European Cup Final against AS Roma. He came on for Johnston and in the penalty shoot-out missed his spot kick. Liverpool nevertheless went on to win the trophy.

Steve figured prominently in the double-winning team of 1986 but only made 14 League appearances the following season. However since then he has been ever-present and has collected another League Championship and FA Cup winners' medal. He has also become an important member of Scotland's national team since making his debut in the 6–1 win over Yugoslavia at Hampden in September 1984.

In his younger days, Steve wanted to be a physical education teacher. But thankfully for Liverpool and Scotland he brought his talents into professional football and today he serves Liverpool as either a solid defender or an attacking midfielder, a position he revels in.

STUART PEARCE

Brian Clough doesn't entrust the captaincy of Nottingham Forest to just any player. But when he gave the job to Stuart Pearce in succession to Ian Bowyer at the start of the 1987–88 season he knew that he had chosen the right man for the job. Tremendously popular with both the fans and his team-mates alike, Stuart was a natural choice for the job, and was a big success in the role.

ENGLAND

STUART PEARCE

Club History
1983–85 Coventry City
1985– Nottingham Forest (£400,000, dual deal)
Honours & Awards
Littlewoods Cup 1989, 1990
Simod Cup 1989

NOTTINGHAM

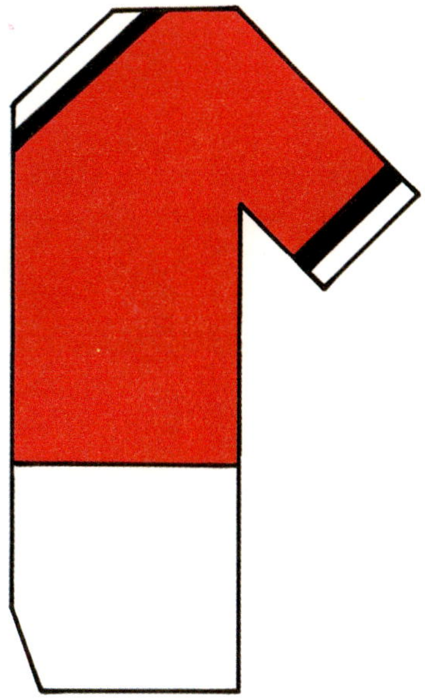

London-born, at Shepherd's Bush, on 24 April 1962, he started his career with Wealdstone before signing for Coventry City in October 1983 in a deal that was worth £25,000 to the Midlands non-leaguers.

He made his League debut for the Sky Blues on 12 November 1983 against Queen's Park Rangers. But after two seasons at Highfield Road, which saw him play 51 League games and score four goals, he was bought by Brian Clough in a £400,000 deal that also included Coventry defender Ian Butterworth.

Butterworth never made it at the City ground and subsequently moved to Norwich. Pearce, on the other hand, became a great favourite and soon settled into the left-back berth.

Having won an England Under-21 cap against Yugoslavia at Peterborough in November 1986, full honours were widely tipped as he gave some outstanding performances for Forest during their League campaign in 1986–87. And at the end of the season he was selected for the senior England team for the first time in the Rous Cup match against Brazil at Wembley.

The following season Forest returned to being the force they had been ten years earlier and challenged Liverpool for the Championship and also reached the semi-final of the FA Cup, only to lose 2–1 to the Anfielders at Hillsborough. Shortly afterwards, Stuart damaged his knee in the international against Hungary and was forced to miss the rest of the season. More important for Bobby Robson, he was also forced to miss the European Championship in Germany, which, perhaps, contributed to England's dismal performance.

Fit for the start of the next season, Stuart only missed a couple of matches as Forest finished third in the Championship, reached the FA Cup semi-final again, but this time there was a trophy for Forest and Stuart as they beat Luton Town 3–1 to win the Littlewoods Cup at Wembley. Three weeks later Forest beat Everton 4–3 in a thriller, also at Wembley, to win the Simod Cup.

Despite his defensive role, Stuart is also capable of scoring goals. His leadership skills also contribute towards making him one of the best all-round players in the English game.

DAVID PLATT

What do current England internationals David Platt and Peter Beardsley have in common? Answer, they were both rejected by Manchester United, and both went on to become £1 million rated footballers.

ENGLAND

DAVID PLATT

Club History
1984–88 Crewe Alexandra
1988– Aston Villa (£200,000)
Honours & Awards
Second Division (runners-up) 1988
PFA Player of the Year 1990

ASTON VILLA

David was born at Chadderton, near Oldham, in 1966 and had a spell at Old Trafford as a junior, but never played in the first team. United released him in 1984 and he moved to Crewe Alexandra where he was given his first chance of League football by manager Dario Gradi.

Platt had ambitions to become a striker but Gradi knew he wasn't strong enough for that role and moulded him for a midfield position. It was in midfield that he made his League debut at home to Mansfield Town on 26 January 1985. He didn't miss another game all season and scored five goals.

Over the next two and a half seasons at Gresty Road he missed just seven more League games and in 1986–87 notched up 23 goals, to make him the third highest scorer in the Fourth Division.

Dario Gradi has been a big influence on David's career and in 1988 when several clubs, including Aston Villa, Watford and Hibernian were interested in signing him, manager Gradi advised him to join Villa.

The move has proved to be the spring-board David needed. He is full of admiration of the work Graham Taylor does for the club, as both manager and coach, and he acknowledges Taylor's contribution towards his own development.

When David joined Villa they were in the Second Division promotion race and he contributed to their eventual return to the First Division, despite a few shaky results towards the end of the season. David's goal in the 1–0 win over fellow title-chasers Bradford City, in front of 36,000 Villa fans in the penultimate match of the season, was the goal that ultimately clinched promotion.

Villa spent their first season back in the top flight consolidating. David scored seven goals in the League but netted six in the Little-woods Cup, including four in the 6–2 win against Ipswich Town. He also scored one goal in the FA Cup as Villa came back from 2–0 down to win 3–2 at . . . Crewe. There's gratitude for you!

Graham Taylor has bought wisely and built his team at Villa and they showed in 1989–90 that they are a team to be reckoned with in the 1990s. David Platt figures prominently in any future plans that Taylor may have, just as he does in Bobby Robson's plans, because he is now a member of the full England squad.

FRANK RIJKAARD

The careers of Ruud Gullit and Frank Rijkaard have taken similar paths. Both were born in Surinam, both played in the same Dutch team as amateurs (DWS of Amsterdam), both played in the same Dutch school team, and of course both now play for AC Milan. The two men also made their international debut against Switzerland on 1 September 1981 when Gullit came on as a substitute for Rijkaard. Both are extremely talented footballers. But unlike Gullit, who is the motivation behind the Milan midfield and attack, Rijkaard is the man who stabilises the defence.

Born in 1962 he followed his father's

HOLLAND

FRANK RIJKAARD
Club History
1979–88 Ajax
1988– Real Zaragoza
1988– AC Milan
Honours & Awards
Dutch League 1980, 1982
Dutch Cup 1986
European Championship 1988
European Cup 1989

A C MILAN

footsteps and entered the world of professional football and joined Ajax. He was in the first-team at the age of 17 playing alongside the likes of Lerby, Arnesen and Krol. But, despite that seemingly auspicious start to his career, the road to the top was far from easy for Rijkaard.

Although he was an established international he went through a bad patch between 1983 and 1985 and was out of the Ajax team. Things were so bad that he was even offered to FC Groningen on loan, but they didn't want him.

When Johann Cruyff returned to Ajax, Frank was re-discovered and earned a recall to the national squad in 1985. However, it all went wrong for Rijkaard once more when it was discovered he was having secret talks with PSV Eindhoven in 1987 about a possible move. This led to him and manager Cruyff falling out and once more he was out of the team.

Cruyff sacked him but he kept in training with the Dutch FA at Zeist before moving to Sporting Lisbon in January 1988. However, they were not given permission to play him so he moved across the border to Spain where he played with Real Zaragoza for ten games.

Frank Rijkaard was in the wilderness. He had no club and his international career seemed doomed. But he was given another lease of life when Holland team manager Rinus Michels brought him into the team for the European Championship and gave him the role of sweeper. He was superb, and suddenly the fortunes of Frank Rijkaard were on the up again.

He gave some great performances and it was unfortunate that he gave away the penalty which allowed West Germany to take the lead in the semi-final. But thankfully Holland pulled back to win 2–1 and earn a place in the final against the Soviet Union. And Frank got the winners' medal his, and his team-mates', performances deserved.

The European Championship was a shop window and after his performances AC Milan took him to Italy, and further glory followed for the tall defender when he starred in the Milan team which beat Steau Bucharest 4–0 to win the 1989 European Cup. A little over 12 months earlier Rijkaard was clubless. What a difference a year makes!

BRYAN ROBSON

The talents of Bryan Robson lie both in his ability to command a game from midfield and his skills as a great leader and captain.

Robson has been one of the successes of the many teams moulded by England manager Bobby Robson (no relative) and when Bryan is missing from either the England or Manchester United team, his is a notable absence.

Born at Chester-le-Street, County Durham, on 11 January 1957, he stood just 5ft 2in and weighed a mere 7st at the age of 15. He was already a talented footballer but his size was a handicap and because of it he

ENGLAND

BRYAN ROBSON

MANCHESTER UTD

Club History
1975–81 West Bromwich Albion
1981– Manchester United (£1,500,000)
Honours & Awards
FA Cup 1983, 1985, 1990

couldn't get into the Durham schoolboy team.

However, he was recommended to West Bromwich Albion and they were prepared to give the frail-looking youngster a trial. They liked what they saw and took him on their books where he served his apprenticeship.

Albion's first priority was to build him up physically, which they did, and on 12 April 1975 he made his Football League debut in a Second Division match with York City. However he received a severe setback in 1976–77 when his future development was hampered by a broken leg.

Bryan has since suffered many injuries which have kept him out of the game for a while. But one of Bryan Robson's greatest assets is determination and in 1976–77 he came back to become a regular at the Hawthorns.

He helped Albion's push towards the First Division title in 1980–81, when they finished fourth but in September 1981 he played his final game for West Brom at Everton. Two weeks later he turned out for his new club, Manchester United, in the local 'derby' with Manchester City.

Ron Atkinson, Robson's boss at Albion, had been appointed United manager in the 1981 close season and he saw Robson as the man to lead United. A few months later a cheque for £1.5 million ensured that Bryan Robson became a Manchester United player.

Robson established a great partnership with fellow England international Ray Wilkins, but at the same time displayed tremendous individual talents in defence, as a creative midfielder, and as a goal scorer.

He led United to victory over Brighton in the 1983 FA Cup Final, and scored two of their four goals in the replay at Wembley. He climbed up Wembley's steps as United captain again two years later when they beat Everton 1–0. But the following year Bryan was plagued with injury. Once again, however, his determination carried him through and he has now gone on to play more than 650 games at senior level and is rapidly approaching his 100th England cap.

He still has a few years of top class football left in him and Bryan Robson would dearly love to get his hands on two trophies – the League Championship trophy as United skipper, and the FIFA World Cup as England captain.

DAVID ROCASTLE

ENGLAND

DAVID ROCASTLE

Club History
1984– Arsenal
Honours & Awards
Milk Cup 1987
League Championship 1989

ARSENAL

A skilful player who operates on the right of midfield, David Rocastle does not score many goals but he certainly creates a lot of chances for his team-mates.

Since coming into the Arsenal side as a youngster he has shown himself to be an outstanding prospect and has gained full international honours with England.

Born in Lewisham, London, in 1967 he came through the apprentice ranks at Highbury and made his debut in the goal-less draw with Newcastle at Highbury on 28 September 1985 as a replacement for Stewart Robson. The following season he was given his chance of regular first-team football and hasn't let go of it.

He helped Arsenal to the Milk Cup final in 1987, when they beat Liverpool 2–1, and returned to Wembley the following year but this time it was a loser's medal for Rocastle as Luton Town spoilt Arsenal's chance of a double success.

When Arsenal won the League title at the last gasp in 1989, David was ever present during the run-in to the title and scored six goals. He was a very important member of a well-balanced team and his midfield contribution for striker Alan Smith was a crucial one.

David was being groomed for international football and made his debut for the England Under-21 team against Sweden in 1986. He has played for the Under-21s on 14 occasions and even captained the side. He made his full international debut against Denmark at Wembley in the wake of England's European Championship failure.

Injuries to Chris Waddle and John Barnes hastened Rocastle's debut but he did his manager and country proud and showed no signs of nerves as he took on the Danish defenders. The Wembley crowd certainly warmed to the debutant.

With a wealth of talent in midfield in the English game, David certainly has to fight for his place in Bobby Robson's team. He is a regular member of the squad, but with age on his side he should one day establish himself as a regular member of the team.

His ability to take on and beat defenders, coupled with his ball control and speed, have made David Rocastle one of the most exciting prospects in the First Division.

ROMARIO

BRAZIL

ROMARIO

PSV EINDHOVEN

Club History
1982–88 Vasco da Gama
1988– PSV Eindhoven (£3,000,000)
Honours & Awards
South American Championship 1989
Dutch League 1989

Brazilian football has been amongst the most exciting in the world since the days when they introduced us to Pele more than 30 years ago. Since then, Brazil has produced a long line of outstanding players who have thrilled footballing fans the world over. The latest star to emerge out of that great country is Romario, a goal-scoring sensation.

Born in January 1966, he started his career with Brazilian League side Vasco da Gama. He made his international debut when he came on as substitute for the Newcastle star Mirandhina in the 69th minute against the Republic of Ireland at Dublin on 23 May 1987. Those amongst the disappointing 18,000 crowd were fortunate to get a glimpse of a rare footballing talent that was about to explode over the next couple of years.

But the footballing fans of Seoul for the 1988 Olympics caught a glimpse of that talent.

Romario was the tournament's top scorer with seven goals as Brazil reached their second successive final. But as in 1984 it was defeat again, this time at the hands of the Russians, who won 2–1 after extra time. Brazil's goal was predictably scored by Romario.

By the time the 1988–89 season came around, Romario had followed his Brazilian team-mate Careca to Europe. But unlike Careca who went to Napoli, Romario signed for PSV Eindhoven in a £3 million deal. He played just 24 games for PSV during the season, but ended up as the Dutch League's top scorer with 24 goals.

He returned to Brazil for the South American Championship and scored the only goal of the final against Uruguay in front of 178,000 fervent fans in Rio to give Brazil its first championship since 1949.

Romario has a remarkable goal-scoring talent and along with his fellow striker Careca has brought back happy memories of those heady days of Jairzinho and Pele. Brazilian football is buzzing once more, thanks largely to the explosive goal-scoring talents of Romario.

IAN RUSH

It took Ian Rush a while to recapture his goal-scoring magic upon his return to Liverpool from Italy. But the Liverpool fans knew that Rush wouldn't be out of the goal-scoring limelight for long.

Probably the most lethal scorer of goals in the 1980s, his talent was spotted while playing for Chester in the late 1970s. But the excellent Liverpool scouting system rarely allows players of Rush's ability to slip through their network, particularly when they are playing their football so close to the Anfield ground. And he eventually signed for Liverpool.

Born in the picturesque town of St Asaph in North Wales on 20 October 1961, Rush was an apprentice with Chester when he made his Football League debut in a Third Division game against Sheffield Wednesday on 28 April 1979. Even Rush couldn't have believed that 12 months later he would be a Liverpool player. But he was.

Bob Paisley paid £300,000 for the 18-year-old after he had scored 14 goals in 34 games for the Sealand Road club. Despite the signing, he remained with Chester until the end of the season before becoming a member of the Anfield set-up. Even before he had kicked a ball for Liverpool he was picked for Wales and won his first full cap in May 1980.

Liverpool have a reputation for not letting youngsters go straight into the first-team. They like them to first get used to the atmosphere of the club, and Rush was treated no differently, despite his obvious talent.

He spent two seasons in the reserves, apart from a handful of first-team games, including an appearance in the replayed Milk Cup final against West Ham in 1981 and the European Cup semi-final against Bayern

WALES

IAN RUSH

Club History
1978–80 Chester
1980–87 Liverpool (£300,000)
1987–88 Juventus (£3,200,000)
1988– Liverpool (£2,800,000)
Honours & Awards
Football League Cup/Milk Cup 1981–84
League Championship 82, 83, 84, 86, 90
PFA & FWA Footballer of the Year 1983
PFA Young Player of the Year 1983
European Cup 1984
Adidas Golden Boot Winner 1984
FA Cup 1986, 1989

LIVERPOOL

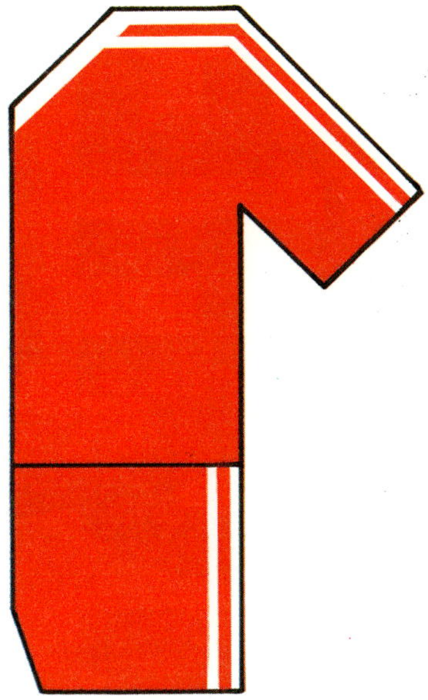

Munich. However, in nine first-team games he had failed to score and there were those pundits who thought he was too ungainly for a striker and doubted the shrewdness of the move. But how wrong they were.

Rush became a first-team regular the following season and netted 30 goals in 48 matches. Those same pundits were now hailing him as one of the greatest strikers in the modern era. And he had even more to offer.

He was the club's top scorer in 1981–82 and collected a championship medal and scored in the Milk Cup final win over Spurs. He was the top scorer again in 1982–83, including a staggering four goals against neighbours Everton. Rush enjoys scoring against the Blues and has since gone on to break Dixie Dean's long-standing record for goals in 'derby' matches. Rush added to his medal tally in 1983 with further League Championship and Milk Cup medals.

It is hard to imagine that he could better his goal-scoring exploits – but he did in 1983–84 when he scored 32 League goals, including five in one game against Luton. This time his goals contributed to the League Championship, Milk Cup *and* European Cup.

Another League Championship, and the FA Cup came Rush's, and Liverpool's way in 1986 but after a blank year in 1986–87 the Welshman had decided on a move to Italian club Juventus. And despite pleas from the Anfield fans to stay, including a suggested collection to pay him increased wages, he made the move to Italy. But it turned out to be disastrous. His goal-scoring touch which brought him 200 goals in 300 games for Liverpool deserted him and he had an unhappy spell abroad.

Kenny Dalglish swooped to bring 'Rushie' back to Anfield in the summer of 1988 when he paid £2.8 million for him – the deal gave Liverpool a profit of £400,000 on the deal. But more importantly, the fans were delighted – and so was Rush.

He struggled at first to find the net, and injury problems from his Juventus days followed him back to Anfield. But just when he was being written off, and only just selected for the 1989 FA Cup final against Everton, he scored two crucial goals in the Reds' 3–2 win which re-affirmed him as one of the most lethal strikers in front of goal.

HUGO SANCHEZ

Hugo Sanchez was the top scorer in the Spanish League in the four consecutive seasons from 1984–85. No other man can make such a claim. And when you consider that some of the world's greatest players, like Di Stefano, Puskas, Ghento and Cruyff have all displayed their talents in Spain, it puts into perspective the magnitude of Hugo Sanchez's goal-scoring exploits.

Born in Mexico in July 1958, he comes from a sporting family. His father, Hector, was a Mexican First Division footballer with Atlante. His brother Horacio was the

MEXICO

HUGO SANCHEZ

Club History
1976–81 Universitario
1981–85 Athletico Madrid (£300,000)
1985– Real Madrid (£1,500,000)
Honours & Awards
Spanish League 1986, 87, 88, 89, 90
UEFA Cup 1986
Spanish Cup 1989

REAL MADRID

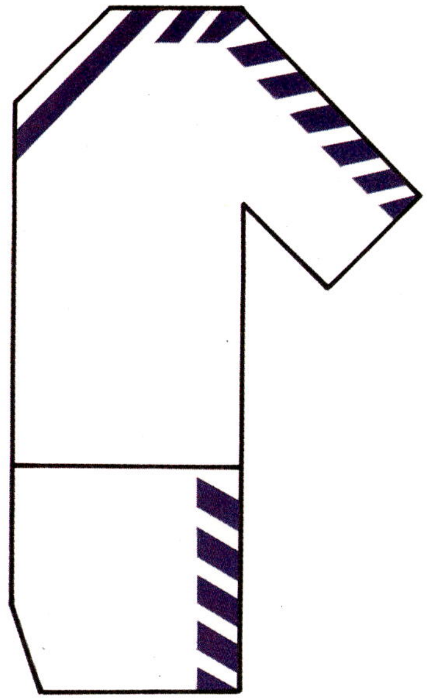

Mexican goalkeeper in the 1972 Olympics. And to continue the line, his sister Herlinda was a gymnast at the 1976 Olympics . . . but wasn't capable of challenging the mighty Nadia Comaneci.

Hugo was playing for Universitario of Mexico City when he made his international debut and at the age of 20 was in Mexico's 1978 World Cup squad. Despite finishing bottom of their group, Sanchez played in all three matches and gave a good account of himself. He has since gone on to win more than 40 Mexican caps.

The 5ft 8in tall Sanchez was signed by Athletico Madrid in 1981 for the bargain fee of £300,000, and in the 1984–85 season he attracted a lot of attention when he headed the Spanish League goal-scoring list, albeit with 19 goals. The mighty Real Madrid saw Sanchez as the replacement for Santillana and out came the cheque book. Mind you, by today's standards, the £1.5 million they had to pay was not excessive.

He slotted into the Real style of play immediately. It suited his game and he scored 22 goals to top the League list for the second successive season. He also collected the first of four consecutive Spanish League winners' medals and scored one of Real's goals in their 5–1 demolition of Cologne in the first leg which took the UEFA Cup to Madrid.

Now hailed as a superstar, Hugo wanted to do well for his home country in the 1986 World Cup which was being staged in Mexico. But he disappointed the home fans. He returned to Mexico a hero, but left a disaster. However, he left with the promise that he would make amends in 1990. Sadly for him, Mexico were thrown out of the tournament after fielding over-age players in a FIFA youth tournament.

After his disastrous World Cup it was back to domestic duties and his 34 goals helped Real to another League title. It was the same story again in 1987–88. Real were champions and Hugo Sanchez was the League's top scorer. Real completed the double in 1989 but Sanchez's 29 goals were bettered by Baltazar's 35.

Hugo Sanchez loves scoring goals. And you always know when he has scored one – he does that distinctive handstand. When he finishes scoring goals he can always turn to his second profession – he is a qualified dentist.

DEAN SAUNDERS

When your dad has played for Liverpool, and in the same team as the legendary Billy Liddell, it's a good bet that you will have the 'football bug'. That's what happened to Dean Saunders.

His father, Roy, was a member of the Liverpool team in the 1950s before his eventual transfer to Swansea Town. And it was in Swansea that Dean was born in 1964.

WALES

DEAN SAUNDERS

DERBY CO

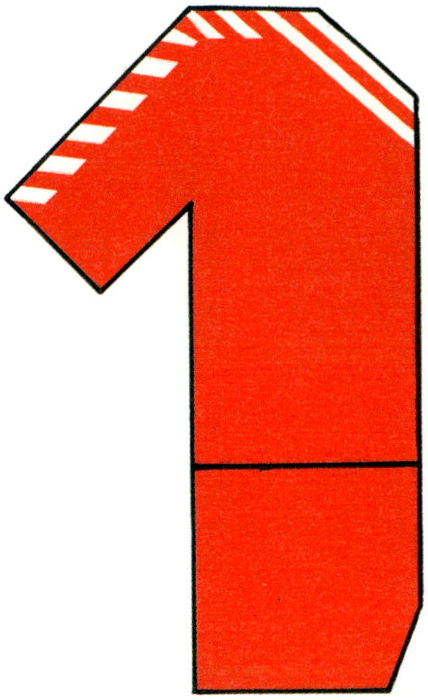

Club History
1982–85 Swansea City
(loan to Cardiff City 1985)
1985–87 Brighton & Hove Albion (free)
1987–88 Oxford United (£60,000)
1988– Derby County (£1,000,000)
Honours & Awards
None, as yet

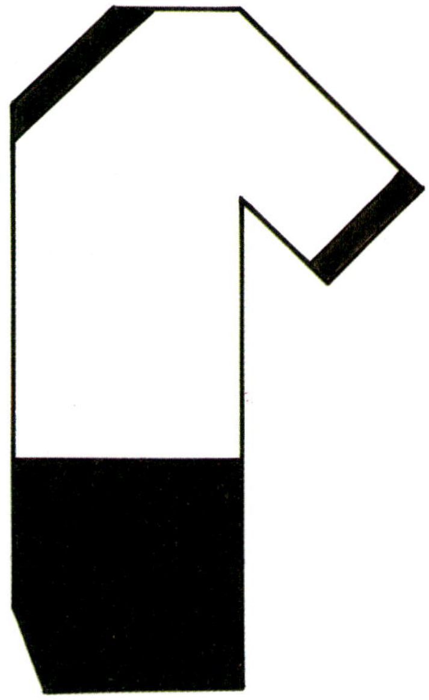

Dean started his career with his home-town team, now re-named Swansea City. Sadly he joined them shortly after their dramatic rise to the First Division from the Fourth. When Dean made his League debut City were on the road back to the Fourth Division.

He made his League debut as a substitute against Charlton in October 1983, but it was not until the latter part of the season that he gained a regular first-team place. He scored three goals in the last ten games, including two in the local 'derby' against Cardiff, but his arrival could not prevent Swansea's drop for the second successive season and they were on their way into the Third Division.

Despite being City's top scorer the following season, he was loaned to Cardiff City shortly after the arrival of John Bond as manager in December 1984. At the end of the season the Swans narrowly missed relegation again but, despite his goal-scoring ability, Dean was given a free transfer and joined Brighton.

It was after his move to the south coast club that his fortunes took a turn for the better. He scored 19 goals in his first season at the Goldstone and gained his first senior Welsh cap against the Republic of Ireland in Dublin on a day that saw Ray Houghton and John Aldridge also make their debuts.

Oxford United signed Saunders just before transfer deadline day 1987 and they saw him as the player likely to help them maintain their First Division status. He did just that by scoring two vital goals in the penultimate match of the season against Luton which guaranteed their First Division status. The £60,000 investment really paid off.

The following season, despite being United's top scorer, it was the drop for Oxford. But after only ten games in the Second Division he returned to First Division football after Derby County paid £1 million for him. It was the deal which resulted in Oxford manager Mark Lawrenson being sacked after a dispute with the board of directors.

But at Derby he has become a firm favourite and his 14 goals helped Derby to fifth place in the League in his first full season at the Baseball Ground. His goal-scoring skills have caused other First Division managers to take note.

PETER SHILTON

To remain at the top of domestic and international football beyond a 40th birthday is a remarkable achievement. But England's Peter Shilton is still regarded as one of the finest goalkeepers in the world despite reaching that particular milestone.

Testament to his ability to stay at the top lies in his complete dedication, professionalism, and desire to train regularly, something he has always enjoyed. Even as a youngster in his early days as understudy to Gordon Banks at Leicester City, he would spend many extra hours at the practice ground developing skills which have since made him the finest 'keeper in the world. And more importantly, kept him at that level for 20 years.

Born in Leicester on 18 September 1949 he joined his home-town team as an apprentice at the age of 16. It was after Banks' transfer to Stoke City in 1967 that 'Shilts' became the regular between the posts at Filbert Street. Two years later he played at Wembley in the FA Cup Final against Manchester City. But sadly for

ENGLAND

PETER SHILTON

Club History
1966–74 Leicester City
1974–77 Stoke City (£340,000)
1977–82 Nottingham Forest (£270,000)
1982–87 Southampton (£325,000)
1987– Derby County (£90,000)
Honours & Awards
Second Division 1971
League Championship 1978
PFA Player of the Year 1978
Football League Cup 1979
European Cup 1979, 1980
European Super Cup 1980
PFA Merit Award 1990

DERBY co

Leicester and Shilton it was Leicester's fourth defeat in as many attempts at trying to win the famous trophy.

In November 1970 Shilton made his international debut in England's 3–1 win over East Germany. But it took some time before he made the England jersey his own property. Throughout the 1970's he shared the jersey with Liverpool's Ray Clemence. But Shilton eventually became the more dominant and has made the position his own since the early 1980s, and he has missed very few games since.

Shilton surprised a lot of people by making the same journey as his predecessor, and moved to Stoke City in a £340,000 deal in 1974. Three years later he was off again, this time to Nottingham Forest in a move that was valued at £270,000. In an era of £1 million transfers, Shilton was an excellent buy for Forest manager Brian Clough. The move paid dividends for both player and club as Shilton collected a personal tally of a League Championship medal, two European Cup winners' medals, a European Super Cup winners' medal, and a winners' medal in the Football League Cup.

After five seasons at Forest he moved to the south coast and joined Southampton before moving back to the Midlands in 1987 when he joined Derby County.

He made his Football League debut against Everton on 4 May 1966, and on 30 April 1988 he established a new Football League record when he broke Terry Paine's long-standing record of 828 appearances. But the record breaking didn't stop there.

He went on to win his 100th England cap against Holland in the 1988 European Championship in Germany, and against Denmark in June 1989 he won his 109th cap to surpass Bobby Moore's England record. Shilton is still adding to that total.

Peter Shilton is one of the game's great ambassadors. He was recognised for his services to the game in 1978 when he was voted Player of the Year by his fellow professionals.

Despite passing the age of 40, he is playing as well as ever. The many up-and-coming young goalkeepers are going to have to bide their time before taking the England jersey from him. Shilts isn't going to give it up that easily.

NEVILLE SOUTHALL

Neville Southall is one of Britain's finest goalkeepers and ranks alongside the great Peter Shilton. Like Shilton, he has got to the top by hard work and perseverance, because the road to the top was no easy one for Welsh-born Southall. A former hod-carrier, he started his career in non-league football and then worked his way through the lower divisions before getting his break into the big time with Everton. And that all came within a remarkable two year spell.

Southall was born in the North Wales seaside town of Llandudno on 16 September 1958 and as a youngster played as a centre-back with local clubs and even had trials as an out-fielder with Crewe Alexandra and Bolton Wanderers. Both trials were unsuccessful. But it was after joining Llandudno Swifts that he turned his attentions to goal-keeping and after brief spells with Conway United and Bangor City he moved to the Cheshire League team Winsford United. In June 1980 he joined Bury for £6,000 and the Football League career of Neville Southall was under way.

He made his debut the following September against Wigan Athletic and thereafter was ever-present that season. Howard Kendall was impressed with Southall and in the 1981 close season bid £150,000, which Bury duly acccepted. At first he was understudy to Jim Arnold at Goodison.

Having made his debut in the 2–1 win over Ipswich Town in October 1981 he was back

WALES

NEVILLE SOUTHALL

Club History
1980–82 Bury (£6,000)
1981– Everton (£150,000)
(Loan to Port Vale 1983)
Honours & Awards
FA Cup 1984
FWA Footballer of the Year 1985
League Championship 1985, 1987
European Cup Winners' Cup 1985

EVERTON

in the reserves. But after being recalled for the 2–0 win over Aston Villa on 19 December he retained his place for the rest of the season. He also won his first full cap for Wales.

However, Neville lost his place after three months of the 1982–83 season and spent part of the season on loan to Port Vale. It looked as though the First Division career of Neville Southall was over. But the man who had only a couple of years earlier been playing non-league football came back and was to become a crucial part of the Howard Kendall team that emerged from the shadow of their more illustrious Merseyside neighbours, Liverpool.

Neville replaced Jim Arnold after a month of the 1983–84 season and has been the regular 'keeper at Goodison ever since.

When he reclaimed his place, Everton were in all sorts of trouble. They were 13th in the table and had won just two of their first seven League games. By the time the New Year came around, Everton's Championship season was well forgotten and Howard Kendall's future as Everton manager was far from secure. But then came two remarkable Cup runs, aided by some outstanding goal-keeping by Southall who confirmed himself as one of the most agile of 'keepers with terrific skills in the air.

Everton reached the Milk Cup final but lost in a replay to Liverpool. Six weeks later they were back at Wembley and this time it was glory as Everton beat Elton John's Watford 2–0 to win the FA Cup. Kendall's job was saved, and glory days returned to one of the game's great clubs.

For Southall it was just reward for his patience and the following year there were even greater glories ahead for Neville and Everton.

He was voted the Football Writers' Player of the Year after he played a crucial role in helping Everton to win their first Championship for 15 years, and also helped them to their first European glory when they won the Cup Winners' Cup. Only a Norman Whiteside goal prevented Everton completing the League and Cup double.

Howard Kendall has since left Everton and been replaced by Colin Harvey. But Neville Southall still figures very prominently in the new manager's plans. But there again, how could a world class goalkeeper like Neville Southall ever be ignored?

CHRIS WADDLE

It is just over ten years since the League career of Chris Waddle was launched. But what a decade it has been for the north-easterner who, in 1989, became one of the world's most expensive footballers when he moved from Tottenham Hotspur to the wealthy French club Marseille for £4.25 million.

In the time since he made his League debut as a youngster with Newcastle, Waddle has become one of England's established internationals.

Chris was born in Hepworth, near Gateshead, in 1960. Ironically, Gateshead's football team lost its League status that same year when they were replaced by Peterborough United.

After being spotted while playing for one of the top local non-league teams, Tow Law Town, Chris was signed by Newcastle United in the summer of 1980 for £10,000.

His League debut was in a Second Division clash with Shrewsbury Town at St James's

ENGLAND

CHRIS WADDLE

Club History
1980–85 Newcastle United (£10,000)
1985–89 Tottenham Hotspur (£500,000)
1989– Marseille (£4,250,000)
Honours & Awards
FA Cup (runner-up) 1987

MARSEILLE

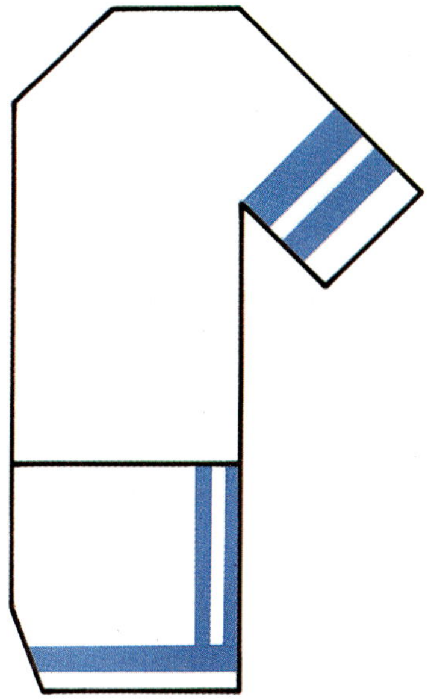

Park on 22 October 1980. He played only 12 more games that season and netted his first goal in the 1–0 win over Queen's Park Rangers on 7 February 1981.

Newcastle boss Arthur Cox was building a team of youth and experience at Newcastle, and Waddle was given his chance of a regular first-team place the following season when he was ever-present and scorer of seven League goals. The Newcastle jigsaw was complete in the 1982–83 season when Cox signed Kevin Keegan and his experience, along with that of Terry McDermott's, allied to the youthful approach of Waddle helped to mould a team that was ready for promotion. It didn't come that first season, but in 1984 Newcastle returned to their rightful place amongst the elite of English soccer.

Keegan was inspirational as a leader and goal-scorer, but so too were Peter Beardsley and Chris Waddle. Between them the three men scored 65 League goals (Chris scored 18) as Newcastle finished third and gained promotion.

Waddle was receiving rave notices from most grounds he appeared on. But how would he figure in the First Division? That was a question that he would soon answer. In 36 games in the top division, Waddle scored 13 goals. The answer was simple. He could cope well. Furthermore, he gained his first and only England Under-21 cap that season, but senior honours were not too far away and in March 1985 he won his first full cap in the 2–1 win over the Republic of Ireland.

Although not a regular goal-scorer for the England team he has been utilised by England manager Bobby Robson down the wing and feeds target men like Gary Lineker. He is at his most dangerous when running at opponents. In the six years since he first pulled on an England shirt, Chris has gone on to win more than 50 caps.

Tottenham signed him for £500,000 in the 1985 close season and he spent four years at Spurs before his multi-million-pound transfer to Marseille in 1989. The nearest he came to a domestic honour was in 1987 when Spurs were beaten by Coventry City in the FA Cup final at Wembley. He is hoping that his fortunes will change in France. Considering the money Marseille have spent on players, the honours need to come their way to justify the investment.

WALTER

ZENGA

WALTER ZENGA

Club History
1977– Inter Milan
Honours & Awards
Italian League 1989

ITALY

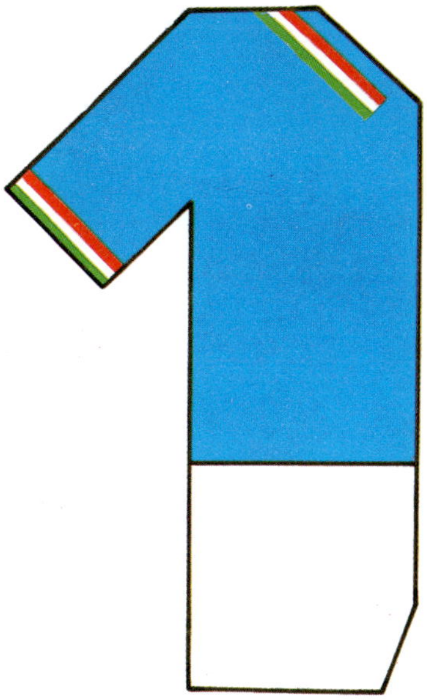

INTER MILAN

When Dino Zoff retired from the international scene after Italy's 1982 World Cup win, the Italian soccer fans must have been wondering if they would ever find such another good goalkeeper. They have been fortunate that Walter Zenga is the man most likely to be between the sticks when Italy returns to the top of the international ladder.

Born in Milan in 1960 he was fortunate to fulfil the dream of 50 per cent of the city's schoolboys by joining Inter Milan as a 17-year-old. He progressed gradually through the youth system as well as being loaned out to a succession of Third Division clubs where he gained valuable experience.

Inter thought he was ready for first-team duty in 1983 and on 11 September he made his senior debut in the 2–1 home defeat by Sampdoria. He replaced Ivano Bordon who had moved to Sampdoria, and from the day of his debut Zenga became a first-team regular.

He has outstanding reflexes and is very steady and has proved himself an adequate replacement for Zoff.

Zenga gained valuable World Cup experience in 1986 when he travelled with the Italian squad to Mexico. Along with Franco Tancredi he was one of Italy's reserve 'keepers. Neither got a game because they were kept out of the team by the more experienced Giovanni Galli.

The tournament was a disaster for Italy when they were ousted at the quarter-final stage by France. Nevertheless, Walter learned a lot from the trip and upon the team's return from Mexico, Zenga replaced Galli and has since been a virtual ever-present in the national side. With more than 30 caps to his credit, Walter Zenga is now a key member of the Italian squad and he is one of the players the Italian fans are confident will help Italy to many future successes.

Sadly, despite his great skills, domestic honours have not been all that forthcoming and it was not until the 1988–89 season, when Inter won the Italian League, that he collected his first domestic medal. His contribution to their successful season was immense and he conceded only 17 goals in 34 games. This is the sort of record the great Dino Zoff would have been proud of.

DEAN SAUNDERS

NEVILLE SOUTHALL

RIC

DAVID ROCASTLE

ROMARIO

G

DA PLA

GARY LINEKER

MARCO VAN BASTEN

STUART

MARK HUGHES

PETER SHILTON

OLEG KUZNETSOV

ALLY McCOIST

DIEGO MARADONA

ST

NI

PAUL